Hiking
Exploring

Gary Davis

Copyright © 2023 Lost In The Ozarks

All rights reserved.

CONTENTS

1	ANTENNA PINE OVERLOOK	4
2	BEAR CREEK CANYON	6
3	BIG CREEK CAVE FALLS	9
4	BOWER'S HOLLOW FALLS	14
5	BUZZARDS ROOST TRAIL	16
6	CECIL COVE LOOP TRAIL – THUNDER CANYON FALLS	19
7	COMPTON'S DOUBLE FALLS	22
8	EDEN FALLS – LOST VALLEY TRAIL	25
9	ELISE FALLS	28
10	INDIAN CREEK TRAIL – EYE OF THE NEEDLE	30
11	FALLING WATER FALLS	32
12	FERN FALLS	34
13	GLORY HOLE FALLS	36
14	GOAT TRAIL TO BIG BLUFF	38
15	HEMMED IN HOLLOW FALLS	40
16	INDIAN ROCKHOUSE TRAIL	42
17	KING'S BLUFF/PEDESTAL ROCKS TRAIL	45
18	KINGS FALLS	47
19	LILES FALLS	48
20	LONESOME HOLLOW FALLS	50
21	LOWER HORSETAIL FALLS	52
22	MAGNOLIA FALLS/WOODS BOYS FALLS/HADLOCK CASCADE	54
23	PAIGE & BROADWATER HOLLOW FALLS	56
24	PARADISE FALLS	59
25	PONCA TO STEEL CREEK – BUFFALO RIVER TRAIL	61
26	RICHLAND FALLS	63
27	RUSH GHOST TOWN TRAIL	65
28	SANDSTONE CASTLE	67

29	SIX FINGER & FUZZY BUTT FALLS	69
30	SMITH CREEK NATURE PRESERVE	71
31	STEELE FALLS	73
32	SWEDEN FALLS	74
33	SYLAMORE CREEK HIKING TRAIL	77
34	TERRY KEEFE FALLS	79
35	TWIN FALLS -CAMP ORR	82
36	TWIN FALLS – RICHLAND CREEK	84
37	TYLER BEND PARK HIKING	86

BONUS ATTRACTIONS

1	ALTHEA SPRING IN OZARK COUNTY MISSOURI	88
2	ARKANSAS GRAND CANYON	91
3	BEAR CREEK OVERLOOK	92
4	BLUE SPRING HERITAGE CENTER	93
5	BLANCHARD SPRINGS	95
6	CITY ROCK BLUFF	97
7	GRAY SPRING	98
8	GRINDERS FERRY	99
9	HODGSON WATER MILL	101
10	MAMMOTH SPRING	103
11	THE PEEL FERRY	105

1
ANTENNA PINE OVERLOOK

GPS COORDINATES

COMPTON TRAIL-HEAD: 36.08119, -93.30326
ANTENNA PINE OVERLOOK: 36.06812, -93.28622

    You begin the hike to Antenna Pine Overlook from the Compton trail-head in Compton Arkansas. This is the trail-head that also includes the hike down to Hemmed In Hollow Falls. This is an overlook of the Buffalo River Valley with amazing views.

    If you search for information on Antenna Pine Overlook online you won't find much detailed info. The small amount we did find wasn't very detailed at all.

    I found that in the past the Boy Scout troops that visited Camp Orr on the Buffalo River would cross the river and make the steep hike up to the overlook. There was an old pine tree there nicknamed Antenna Pine. The scouts would climb the tree and place the flag of their troop at the top of the tree. When another troop found a flag in the top of the tree they would "capture" the flag and return it to camp, replacing the flag with their own.

    The bluff just below the hill where the tree is located has amazing views of the river valley below. You can also see the road leading to Kyle's Landing as well as the Eye of the Needle on the far side of the river.

    There are several ways to reach the overlook. I did find posts saying you can reach it from Erbie Road by parking along the park boundary and coming in from the top. Since we weren't sure that the GPS coordinates we found online were correct we began our hike at the Compton Trail-head. This is the trail-head you would begin the hike to Hemmed In Hollow Falls too, so in warmer weather, the parking area may be crowded. However, on this day at the end of November, we had the whole parking area to ourselves when we arrived just before 9 am.

After a short hike downhill you will reach the Bench Trail that runs along the top of the bluffs surrounding the hollow. Make a left turn at the sign and follow the bench trail.

After a few hundred yards you will come upon a small cabin beside the trail. I saw this mentioned as "Wild Vic's Cabin" online, but I'm not sure this is the name of the cabin. I couldn't find it listed on the Park Service website. In any event, it is a cool old cabin for you to see how people lived in the area in the past.

From this point, the trail to Antenna Pine is around 3 miles. The trail is fairly flat with some great views of the river valley when the leaves are off the trees. There are also bluffs, old rock walls, and other interesting sights along the way.

As you near the bluff the trail has a fork to the left and you can see some orange trail marker ribbon tied along the trail. This trail will take you up to the bluff below Antenna Pine. Follow the bluff to the left, again marked by ribbon and you will reach a spot where you can scramble up by doing some climbing. This point isn't for the faint of heart. The climb is on the bluff face with few spots for hand holds. A fall here could result in a serious injury. This isn't to discourage you from making the climb, but to reiterate that you should be VERY CAREFUL because you are miles from rescue should an injury occur.

2
BEAR CREEK CANYON – OZARK NATIONAL FOREST

GPS COORDINATES

PARKING: 35.68686, -93.17374
SWAMP FALLS: 35.68892, -93.18644

Bear Creek Canyon is located in the Ozark National Forest in north Arkansas. This area is a waterfall lovers' paradise. We viewed 6 distinct waterfalls within a few hundred yards of each other. I will add that this hike was tougher for me than the other hikes we have taken. It is a little less than a mile down to the first waterfall on the trail. The elevation change was noted as 650' on my GPS. It is very steep and at times the trail is very narrow along the bluff line beside the creek.

To reach Bear Creek Canyon take Highway 7 South from Harrison. The drive from Harrison took a little over an hour and a half. Once you reach Sand Gap (still listed on some maps as Pelsor) turn right onto State Highway 123 to the west. Approximately 4.4 miles west, you will see a forest road to the left. There isn't a traditional road sign on the highway, so you want to be looking for a small signpost close to the trees with 1802 on it. That is the road to the trail-head.

This road is a lot better than most of the roads to reach hiking trails in the Ozarks. I had no problem with my 2-wheel drive SUV. If there hasn't been a lot of rain, I would say even passenger cars could easily navigate this road. About 2.2 miles from the highway there will be a small parking area on the left and a few yards further down the road there is a rutted lane that leads into the forest on the right. There is a small sign there like the one on the highway that designates this road as 93179A. This is where you want to begin your hike if you don't have a 4WD vehicle. With a high clearnce vehicle you should be able to reach the clearing a few hundred yards into the woods and park there.

    The trail into Bear Creek Canyon is not a well-worn trail, but it wasn't a complete bushwhack either during this time of the winter. Go to the rear of the small clearing and you will see an upland swamp with a small stream flowing downhill. Cross this stream and begin looking for the trail markers. The trail will lead you down to the top of Swamp Falls. From here you can also see Sidewinder Falls just a short distance upstream. In warmer weather, I can see how the briers and other sticking weeds might make this a lot more of an adventure.

    We chose to cross the creek at this point and head downstream to view the other falls along Bear Creek Canyon before heading upstream. The trail is narrow and slick in this area after a rain, so USE CAUTION! There is a break in the bluff line a few hundred yards down the trail past Slot Pool Falls. On the day we were there, we also had the added enjoyment of viewing an unnamed fall pouring over the bluffs high above and cascading down into Bear Creek.

    Now that you have made it down from the bluffs, you can make your way back upstream to view Slot Pool Falls (AKA Long Slot Falls). If there has been much rain, you will probably get wet crossing the creek. I did get wet feet making this crossing. But the view from below the falls of the beautiful turquoise pool made me forget about my wet feet.

We were unable to get around the falls without getting wet, so we returned up the bluff and headed back the way we came. The trail passes V Slot Falls, and we were able to climb down a little to an outcrop for some photos of the falls from above.

At this time, we followed the trail back to Swamp Falls. From this point, there is a trail beside the creek heading upstream. You can see Sidewinder and Baby Bear Falls from here when the leaves are off the trees. We walked the trail to Baby Bear Falls a few hundred yards and were astonished at another unique waterfall with a gorgeous turquoise pool below it.

We didn't have time to explore more on this trip because we knew we still had a rough hike uphill ahead of us. It is about a mile uphill and the trail is very steep. In my opinion, this hike out was tougher than when we hiked Hemmed In Hollow Falls. It is a shorter distance, but there are very few level stretches on this one. Plan to take several rest stops along the hike out to the parking area.

This should definitely be on the list of every waterfall lover. Go after a rain or during the rainy season to get the best views. Be sure and have a compass or GPS, preferably both, in case your electronics fail for whatever reason. I did note that I received messages on my phone in several spots, so there is spotty cell reception, but once down into Bear Creek Canyon there was no service. This is typical of this area of the Ozarks, so plan accordingly.

3
BIG CREEK CAVE FALLS

GPS COORDINATES

PARKING - 35.87665, -93.15891
BIG CREEK CAVE FALLS - 35.86300, -93.15480
WOLF CREEK CAVE FALLS - 35.86086, -93.15217

Big Creek Cave Falls is located in Newton County, Arkansas. It is one of many gorgeous places to hike in the Ozark National Forest.

To reach Big Creek Cave Falls from the north take Highway 7 South from Harrison through Jasper. About 1.6 miles north of the junction with Highway 16 look for the sign for Newton County Rd. 6840. The sign will be on the left side of the road. The road looks more like the turn onto a farm road that would be private property, but it is a county road. After a few hundred feet the road will open up. If coming up from the south, take Highway 7 about 1.6 miles north from the Highway 16 junction, and the sign will be on your right.

If you look on Google Earth for the road it is still marked as County Road 59. Keep that in mind if you print out a map.

The road down to the parking area for Big Creek Cave Falls is quite steep and rough in places.

From the highway to the parking area there is about a 1000' elevation change. Rocks jut from the roadbed and I would recommend an SUV to get down there. The road was dry when we visited in early March 2021, so it wasn't too slick. I'm sure it could become slick after a heavy rain, so keep that in mind. It is about 2.8 miles from the highway to the parking area.

Once at the parking area it was time to don our backpacks and head out to see if we could find the falls. Walk around the gate here and begin down the old logging road that is still fairly visible. You will encounter an old homestead, and you'll see a collapsed building and the remains of an old rock wall and cellar.

As you pass this area you will come out into a small open field. You will cross the Right Fork of Big Creek here. I didn't count this as a water crossing since we were able to walk on rocks to cross the creek. Follow the trail here, and continue through the treeline into a larger field. You can follow the old road remnant that is still visible clearly to cross the field. The views of the surrounding hills are quite stunning, so you may be tempted to take a break and stand here for a few minutes to look around.

The road remnant will take you to the far side of the large field, and you will encounter your first water crossing. If you don't want to deal with wet feet for the rest of the hike I suggest bringing along water shoes and taking the time to change into them to make the crossing. I couldn't find any way to jump from rock to rock and not get wet here, so we took the time to change before continuing the hike.

After you cross you will enter another small field. Just follow the road, and you will enter the woods on the far side. Continue to follow the old logging road as it winds along Big Creek. There are a number of side trails you will encounter along the way. These are surrounded by thorny vines so be aware that long pants may keep you from some nasty cuts from those thorns. But the scenes when you go into the creek bed are quite amazing.

You can continue to follow the road along the creek, and you will continue to see amazing views, even from the trail.

After following the road for a while further you will come upon the place where Wolf Creek and Big Creek converge. This is very close to where you take a small side trail to Big Creek Cave Falls.

Someone has kindly placed an orange marker ribbon on a tree, so it is easy to spot the crossing. You will need to break out your water shoes again here to cross Wolf Creek. The trail on the far side of Wolf Creek is the only real climb we encountered on the hike. The trail climbs and goes around Big Creek to Big Creek Cave Falls. Water flows out of a cave in the bluff and falls about 30 feet onto the rocks below. It seems that much of the water goes back underground here. The water flow from the cave was much higher than the amount of water flowing down the hill into the creek bed below. Even though the falls are only 30', they are still very impressive coming out of the opening in the bluff.

After visiting Big Creek Cave Falls we set out to find Wolf Creek Cave Falls. These falls come out of another cave opening.

The trail to Wolf Creek Cave Falls has some interesting things to see. There is a gate on the trail with a chain and lock secured to a tree. But there isn't any type of fencing, so the trail simply goes around the gate. You also pass another interesting formation on the trail up to the falls. The creek runs underground into the rocks below the falls, and the creek disappears underground and it appears at some point to enter the creek below.

On this trip, we also took a side trail at the cattle grate to see the old homestead. There is a rock wall and several old car bodies to be seen just a short hike off the main trail. Be careful because the area is overgrown with briers that have sharp thorns.

If you decide to visit the area just be sure and take a GPS or compass if you plan to get off of the old road. Cell reception is spotty all around this area, so another way of navigation is highly recommended. Spare batteries are also essential. I always carry two spare sets of rechargeable batteries for the GPS, even though I have never had to make use of them. Back country exploring always has the risk of you getting turned around, especially if the weather is cloudy and you can't see the sun. Better safe than sorry.

4
BOWERS HOLLOW FALLS

GPS COORDINATES

**PARKING - 35.86272, -93.46267
BOWERS HOLLOW FALLS – 35.85415, -93.43470**

Bowers Hollow Falls is located in the upper Buffalo River Wilderness. I can say that although we spotted several cars on the way in we had the whole trail to ourselves. Let me just say that this is one of the most strikingly beautiful waterfalls we have visited. It is listed as 56' tall, but it seems taller when you are looking down from the bluffs surrounding the falls.

If coming in from the north use Highway 43 from Harrison to Ponca and the Lost Valley Area. When you reach the intersection of Highway 43 and Highway 21 turn left and travel about 1.2 miles. Then turn right on Cave Mountain Road (County Road 5) at the Hawks Bill Crag sign just before you cross the Buffalo River Bridge.

This road is very steep and rough. It can be very slick in wet weather. It took us 45 minutes to travel a little less than 10 miles to the trail-head. At around the 8.6-mile mark, you will see FR-1410 to the left. Stay on FR-1410 for a little over 1.5 miles. On your left, you will see FR-1410B. If you don't have a 4WD be sure and park here. This also adds about a mile to your hike. However, going past here without a 4WD IS NOT a good idea. The road is rough and muddy and could easily get you stuck without a high-profile vehicle.

At the T in the road, there are a couple of parking spots. There was one truck there when we arrived, so we were able to park there. However, you can drive a short distance to the right at the T and park at Kapark Cemetery. Ken Smith Falls and McClure Falls are also reached on this same trail. We hiked them at a later date, and they are covered later in the book.

This is not a well-worn trail, but it is easy enough to follow. I do recommend a GPS with the coordinates to the falls if you decide to try this one. You can download the GPX file from our website and upload it to your GPS unit and you will have the track we used to reach the falls.

To get below the falls take a trail to your right when you reach the top of the falls. You can walk about a 1/4 mile along the top of the bluff line, and you will find a break in the bluff line where you can scramble down fairly easily. Then you can make your way back along the bluff to get below the falls. We found that staying close to the bluffs is the easiest route to get to the spot below the falls.

Please be aware that this is one of the few places that Google Maps gets wrong. You can see the actual location if you put in the GPS coordinates from above. You will see it on the map if you look up and to the right from the pin. Look for a blue-green pool in the valley along the creek running west to east.

5
BUZZARDS ROOST HIKING TRAIL

GPS COORDINATES

PARKING - 35.63629, -93.15787
BUZZARDS ROOST – 35.63368, -93.13327

    The Buzzards Roost hiking trail and scenic area is located in the Ozark National Forest in Newton County, Arkansas. The trail is basically an old ATV road and is fairly flat.

    To reach the trail-head from the north take Highway 7 south to Sand Gap, also labeled on some maps as Pelsor, Arkansas. At the crossroads of Highway 7 and 123 in Sand Gap turn west and follow Highway 123 for about 4.7 miles. Look for FR 1802 on the left (south side of the road). FR 1802 is a relatively smooth gravel road so it should be passable with most vehicles. You will pass the parking area for the Bear Creek Drainage on the way in. You can read about Bear Creek and the waterfalls there in this article.

    You will reach a fork in the road, and you want to stay left on FR 1805. Follow this until you see a white house on the right that appears abandoned. There is a small parking area on the left beside an old barn.

The distance from Highway 123 to the parking area is about 6.7 miles. I suggest setting your odometer when you turn off the highway. Alternatively, you can enter the coordinates of the parking area into your vehicle's navigation system.

The trail is about 2 miles each way. You can add another 1/2 mile each way if you visit the large natural arch that is a little further along the trail after you visit Buzzards Roost. Below is a photo of the large natural arch.

If you visit the large arch the total distance will come close to 5 miles. But since the trail is mostly flat I would rate this one as easy to moderate.

To reach Buzzards Roost you should take the trail to the right before you get to the large arch. If you decide to see the arch first, just track back along the trail until you see the ATV trail to the left. There aren't any markings but it should be easy to spot. You will reach a large cleared area that appears to be a popular camping spot. The trail starts downhill at the back of this clearing. Just a short distance downhill you will arrive at Buzzards Roost.

Buzzards Roost is a collection of large sandstone rocks with a small arch, amazing views of the valley below, crevasses, and small caves you can explore. You can climb around on the rocks above for views of the hills and valleys. Just be careful as some of the crevices between the rocks are quite deep. You don't want to fall and get a nasty injury back here.

You can go around the rock outcropping to get below and explore the nooks and crannies under, around, and between the rocks. There are plenty of places to explore here.

6
CECIL COVE LOOP – THUNDER CANYON FALLS

GPS COORDINATES

PARKING – 36.08358, -93.23349
THUNDER CANYON FALLS – 36.08427, -93.25465

The Cecil Cove Loop trail makes a slow descent down to Cecil Creek. Along the way, we met a young lady who was walking a small dog. She asked us if we knew where Thunder Canyon Falls was. When we replied that it was our first trip she said she had spoken to quite a few people who had tried and failed to find it. She said she was unable to find the falls as well. Since we hadn't been there before she decided to end her hike and not join us since she wasn't sure we could find it either. But I was confident we could because I had spent some time studying maps and had a pretty good idea of where to look.

At the first crossing, there was a small flow and the water wasn't deep. I had brought a pair of water shoes just in case there was deep water in Cecil Creek. I didn't want to have to make the whole hike with wet feet so bringing water shoes would prevent that. Luckily this wasn't necessary here. It turns out that the flow here was created by the outflow from Van Dyke Spring. The spring is up another creek that runs into Cecil Creek just upstream from here.

After this point, the trail meanders along the creek and is pretty much level. Along this area, you'll get to see bluffs and side creeks that run into Cecil Creek. The trail is mostly wide here because it is also used by horses. Just a warning here to beware of horse droppings on the trail. It isn't pleasant to be walking along and step into a large pile dropped from the back end of a horse.

After a bit, the trail will take you back across Cecil Creek. You should be counting because you want to look for the trail to the falls right after the fourth creek crossing. This is another crossing where you might need to wade water to cross the creek. Fortunately, once again we were able to cross without getting too wet due to the low water level in the creek.

The trail pretty much follows this pattern through the third crossing. The scenery is truly breathtaking with lowland old-growth trees all around you, along with amazing views of the bluffs surrounding you on all sides.

As we approached the fourth crossing I had already spotted where the bluff-line curved to make what looked like a canyon. When we arrived at the final water crossing the water in the creek was running beneath the rocks. That made this one a dry crossing as the rocks were totally dry on top.

Once you make this crossing you want to immediately start looking to your left. This is where the trail branches off into the canyon to Thunder Canyon Falls. There is a tree with a yellow trail marker right beside Cecil Creek Trail. Find that tree and the trail to the falls will be on the left going up the hill.

This is where the trail gets rough. I wouldn't recommend this trail for small children. The trail gets narrow and the rocks and trail get slippery in places. Water seeping from the surrounding rocks makes the trail somewhat muddy. In addition, the smooth rocks down in the creek bed have been worn by eons of erosion.

Cautious and slow are the words of the day as you hike into the canyon where the falls are located.

The smooth areas of the bedrock that are wet are extremely slick. I know because I was trying to get as close to the falls as I could and suddenly found myself on my back on the wet rock. I very nearly smashed the back of my head into the rock when I fell. I'm not sure how I kept my head from striking the rock as it snapped back when I landed.

The falls have worn through the rock and created a narrow slot where the water flows into the creek below. As I said, cautious footwork is vital in this area as the rocks are slick due to the constant water flowing and splashing onto them. Remember that you are over a mile and a half back in the wilderness with no cell service. This would not be a good place for a serious injury because you were being careless. Most people we asked about this hike admitted that they had fallen at least once while near the falls. This is not to discourage you but simply to let you know that caution is necessary when visiting these amazing areas of the Natural State. For more information on Thunder Canyon Falls, you can visit the Buffalo National River website.

7
COMPTON'S DOUBLE FALLS TRAIL

GPS COORDINATES

PARKING – 35.88760, -93.46884
AMBER FALLS – 35.88384, -93.47008
COMPTON'S DOUBLE FALLS - 35.87933, -93.46269
OWL FALLS - 35.87909, -93.46249

    The trail-head for Compton's Double Falls is along Cave Mountain Road in Newton County. If you have ever heard of Whitaker Point/Hawks bill Crag this trail is in the same area. In fact, if you arrive from State Highway 21 as we did, the trail-head is approximately 1.1 miles beyond the trail-head for Whitaker Point. You have to watch closely because the trail-head for Compton's Double Falls isn't well marked and there isn't a parking area, just a slightly wider spot in the road. There was once a sign on the road designating the Upper Buffalo Wilderness/Ozark National Forest, but the only thing left of the sign now is the word, Ozark. If you find the sign, the trail starts right behind it. Also, make sure you don't park blocking the road, as there is a lot of traffic on this road during good weather.

    The hike to Compton's Double Falls is downhill for the first part of the trail. The first 0.3 mile is a pretty steep downhill grade heading in. At the bluff line, there is a fork in the trail. The right fork is a short trail leading down below Amber Falls. Amber falls is a short waterfall with a pool underneath.

After spending a little time at Amber Falls you can scramble back up to the trail and continue on to Compton's Double Falls. After a while following the trail along the bluffs, with the creek on your right, you will come to a drainage coming in from the left. This drainage has a small unnamed fall that you will see as you cross the small trickle of water.

You can cross the creek just below these falls on the rocks and not get your feet wet. Follow the trail around the bluff and there is a spot where I believe you could scramble down and get below this waterfall, but we chose not to do that and continued on to Compton's Double Falls. Continue to follow the trail (it is fairly well-worn) and you will come to the top of Compton's Double Falls beside the trail. You can walk into the stream bed and look over the top of the falls. There are also some interesting cascades above Compton's Double Falls.

Enjoy some time looking around the top of the falls, then rejoin the trail and continue along the bluff line for a short distance. The trail leads downhill at a break in the bluff line. This part of the trail is slick and steep, but if you are cautious you should be fine. Once you get down to the creek bed, find a spot where you can cross on the rocks and cross the creek again. The far side of the creek is a little better walking to get beneath Compton's Double Falls.

We spent some time below the falls drinking some water and resting on the rocks, and then we had one more waterfall to find. If you look just downstream from the point where you crossed the creek there is a drainage to the right. Go into this drainage for about 50 yards and you will find the beautiful cascade waterfall known as Owl Falls. You'll have to climb over some rocks to get there, but it is a breathtaking sight, so be sure and see it if you are already this close.

8
EDEN FALLS – LOST VALLEY TRAIL

GPS COORDINATES

PARKING – 36.01016, -93.37456
EDEN FALLS – 36.01757, -93.38740

The Lost Valley Trail is located on Highway 43 near Ponca, Arkansas in Boxley Valley. You may know Boxley Valley because of the elk that people flock to the area to view. In fact, we were able to see the elk in a field along the highway as we were driving in.

From the parking area, you will see the trail-head along with a pavilion and restrooms. There is a sign at the trail-head that gives you information on the sights you will see on your hike.

The first one-quarter of a mile of the trail is handicap accessible and paved. It is on this section of the trail that you can see the huge limestone boulders which have fallen from the bluffs above Clark Creek. This is called the Jigsaw Blocks. There are huge boulders in and along the creek. As you hike a little further along the trail, you can see the Natural Bridge.

As you continue along the trail from the Natural Bridge you begin ascending a pretty steep part of the trail as the bluff line follows Clark Creek. After a short hike, you will see a trail to your right that leads down to the natural bluff shelter known as Cob Cave. This shelter was so named because in 1931 archaeologists from the University of Arkansas found artifacts, including corn cobs, in the shelter dating back around 2,000 years.

As you explore Cob Cave you will also be able to see Eden Falls. Eden Falls drops from an opening in the rocks above Cob Cave. The waterfall drops in several sections before finally ending in a pretty blue-green pool next to Cob Cave.

Follow the trail back up out of Cob Cave and turn right to get to the top of Eden Falls. This is where the climb gets somewhat tougher. You will need to climb the stone stairs until you reach the top of Eden Falls. This area can be slick so use proper caution.

Now you'll notice that Clark Creek flows out of an entrance in the hillside to create Eden Falls. This is the entrance to Eden Cave. If you follow the cave about 200 feet you will enter a room where there is an underground waterfall.

If you decide to try and enter the cave be sure you have flashlights for each member of your party with fresh batteries. Use caution and don't disturb the natural surroundings. You may even be able to see bats hanging from the ceiling.

Unfortunately, on this trip, I had taken my bright flashlight out of my backpack at home. I was left with a small flashlight that wasn't bright enough to attempt the trip back into the cave. I only managed about 50 feet before having to turn back. On the following page is a photo I got from inside the cave.

9
ELISE FALLS-SMITH CREEK NATURE PRESERVE

GPS COORDINATES

PARKING – 35.93470, -93.38637
ELISE FALLS – 35.93812, -93.38206

Elise Falls is one of the amazing sights you can see if you visit the Smith Creek Nature Preserve. The Smith Creek Nature Preserve is over 1300 acres of Ozark forest preserved to protect the land and wildlife. The preserve is located on State Highway 21 just a few miles south of Ponca, Arkansas.

The Smith Creek Nature Preserve sits atop Sherfield Cave. This cave is home to one of the largest colonies of Indiana Bats in the state of Arkansas. Although the cave is off-limits due to the fragility of the ecosystem it contains, Smith Creek Preserve has a bounty of other sights for you to see.

One of these sights is Elise Falls. From the parking area, the hike down to Elise Falls is about 0.75 miles. The hike down to the falls is pretty much downhill all the way to Smith Creek. Once you reach the creek, the hike levels off and it is a short hike to Elise Falls.

After crossing the creek, look for a lightly used side trail to your left. There will be a small side creek that joins Smith Creek. Elise Falls is about 75 yards up this side creek. The day we were there, we were lucky because there was a small pile of rocks that marked the trail to the left. Otherwise, we would have probably missed it. The falls are around a bend in the creek, which you couldn't see from the main trail.

Crossing the creek was fairly easy on this day because there was only a small amount of water in Smith Creek.

You will see an opening with a small cascade entering Smith Creek from directly in front of you. Walk this small creek a short distance and you will round a bend and there will be Elise Falls.

Watch your step here because the rocks can be slippery.

Once you have hung out at the falls for a while, there is a choice to make. If you decide to go on along the trail you used to get here, there are many more sights. The distance if you decide to make the loop trail hike back to the parking lot is about 2 1/4 miles. The other option is to walk the trail back the way you came.

Since the trail coming down was all downhill, it is all uphill coming back to the parking area. This is why I would rate this trail as moderate to difficult.

10
INDIAN CREEK TRAIL - EYE OF THE NEEDLE

GPS COORDINATES

PARKING – 36.05513, -93.28173
EYE OF THE NEEDLE – 36.02837, -93.28640

The Indian Creek Trail is about 5 miles in and out to the part of the trail where you have to use ropes to ascend the bluff to see Eye of the Needle. This trail is rated moderate to difficult in most online resources, and I would agree. I don't think my legs have ever been this sore after a hike.

The trail-head for the Indian Creek Trail is to the left as you enter the campground at Kyle's Landing. Just follow the road to the left and park at the back of the campground. There is a sign marking the trail-head, and also a map of the area posted. The Indian Creek Trail crosses both the Buffalo River and the Ozark Highlands trails at points near the trail-head Just continue to stay to the left and you will be on the trail.

The weather made for interesting conditions, as the rocks were all coated with condensation from the humidity. This made walking on the smooth rocks a little more treacherous than it would be normally. There were a few slips and falls, but nothing major.

The first part of the trail goes through the bottoms near the Buffalo River. If you observe the trees around you it is easy to see the results as the river rises and rushes through this area. We observed lots of debris caught in the trees along the trail. You wouldn't want to be caught here during a flash flood.

As you continue along the trail you will enter the creek bed of Indian Creek. Following the trail can be challenging at times, as it is not well marked. But if you take your time you can find the route up and around the water and huge boulders along the creek.

After following the trail a little over 2 miles you reach a box canyon and a small waterfall that is coming out of the rocks. This is the point where you need to climb to reach the Eye of the Needle.

This rugged wilderness is amazingly beautiful. There are waterfalls and caves to explore, and you will observe springs flowing from the rocks along the sides of the creek. At many points along the Indian Creek Trail, the water flows underground beneath your feet, only to emerge as it encounters bedrock.

11
FALLING WATER FALLS

GPS COORDINATES

FALLING WATER FALLS – 35.72207, -92.94931

Falling Water falls is one of the easiest waterfalls you can visit in the Ozarks. This waterfall is easy to visit because it is right beside the road. You can drive right up to the falls.

If you are coming from Harrison, AR, you will take Highway 7 south to the junction of Highway 16. Your map may say Pelsor or it may say Sand Gap. This is an unincorporated town according to my research, and the name was changed to Sand Gap. Either way, you will turn right toward Ben Hur on Highway 16.

Just outside the town of Ben Hur, you will see at a small church on the right. You will turn right onto Upper Falling Waters Road. You then simply follow this road to the falls.

Before you arrive at Falling Water Falls, you will see an interesting cascade in the creek on the right side of the road. Be sure and stop there if the water is running. It makes for some great photos.

Whatever you do, don't make the same mistake we did a few years ago and think that these are actually Falling Water Falls. We drove here a few years ago and took some photos. We turned around and drove back the way we came, never suspecting at the time that only about 3/4 of a mile up the road were the true falls. It was only when we were looking at Google Earth while researching that we realized how close we had come. We also knew we had to go back since there has been a lot of rain in the Ozarks this spring. We were not disappointed.

You can drive right up to both of these places of amazing natural beauty in a car. There is no hiking involved whatsoever. The pool below the falls is a popular swimming hole in the summer. If you want to get photos without other people in them, you may have to plan to visit in the off-season. It's also best to plan a visit after significant rainfall, as the flow will diminish during the dry season.

After seeing Falling Water Falls, you could turn around and return the way you came. But if you feel truly adventurous, you should continue to Richland Creek Campground and beyond. Although the road can get steep and winding in places, we did see a sports car very close to the campground. The road seems to be very well maintained.

The drive to the campground has some amazing sights. And if you are interested in seeing more waterfalls, there are 6 Finger Falls and Terry Keefe Falls on the drive to the campground. Once you get to the campground, you can follow a 2 1/2-mile trail to get to Richland Falls.

As always, you want to be careful when you visit these places. There are steep hills, wet and slippery rocks, and other dangers. Just be aware and use common sense. It should also be noted that this is a wilderness area. For most of the drive, we had little to no cell service. It was spotty at best, and most places had no service.

12
FERN FALLS

GPS COORDINATES

PARKING – 35.89290, -93.19026
FERN FALLS – 35.89742, -93.19246

The parking area for Fern Falls is south of Jasper, AR. on Scenic Highway 7. There is an area for parking near the sign for Scenic 7 Byway on the west side of the highway.

Begin the hike to Fern Falls beside the sign and you'll see a trail heading west into the forest. Follow this trail until you reach a fork in the old road trace. Take the right fork and begin a slow downhill descent. As you descend down the trail you will soon see a creek on your left. The trail follows the creek and eventually you will come to another fork in the trail.

Take the right fork a short distance and you can view the falls from above. Once you have viewed the falls from above you can backtrack a short distance and take the fork to the left. Find a place to cross the creek, and follow the trail a short distance. You'll see a break where you can scramble down below the falls and under a bluff shelter. The total distance for this short hike is a little over 1.5 miles round trip.

13
GLORY HOLE FALLS

GPS COORDINATES

**PARKING – 35.82833, -93.39035
GLORY HOLE FALLS – 35.82204, -93.39353**

Glory hole falls is a unique sinkhole waterfall in the Ozark National Forest. The parking area for the falls is along AR Highway 16/21 south of Boxley Valley. There is a small sign and a parking area beside the highway.

According to my GPS, the trail is 1.1 miles in each direction. The trail is mostly downhill to the falls, so this means the trail out is mostly uphill all the way. Although it is uphill hiking back out, it is about a 400' elevation change over a mile, so I still rate this one as easy/moderate, depending on your physical condition.

The total distance we hiked was 2.2 miles, and the beginning elevation at the trail-head for Glory Hole Falls is about 2100 feet above sea level, and Glory Hole Falls is at about 1700' elevation, for about 400' of elevation change.

Glory Hole Falls is unique in that the drainage has worn a hole in the bedrock and the water now drains down through the hole instead of running over the rock ledge above the stream bed below when there is low flow in the creek.

The hike to Glory Hole Falls begins down an old road. A short distance down the trail there is a fork, and there is now a flat rock with an arrow painted on it indicating to take the right fork in the trail. This can be a help to those who aren't as familiar with hiking this trail. The trail continues downhill and you will cross the creek that drains down and creates the falls.

Be sure and spend some time exploring around the falls and below the falls along the creek. The scenery is gorgeous, and there are plenty of sights to see in this rugged area of the Ozarks. Another waterfall not far from here is Paradise Falls, and the Smith Creek Conservation Area is only a short drive north of here toward Boxley Valley.

14
GOAT TRAIL TO BIG BLUFF

GPS COORDINATES

PARKING – 36.06410, -93.36046
BIG BLUFF GOAT TRAIL – 36.05237, -93.32306

The Big Bluff Goat Trail is a spur trail off the Centerpoint Trail in the Ponca Wilderness of the Buffalo National River. You start your hike at the Centerpoint trail-head next to Highway 43 at Compton, AR. This trail gets crowded during warmer weather. If you get there and the lot is full, you can park across the highway where a sign is posted. Parking there will cost you $5, so you might want to get to the parking area early.

From the trail-head, the trail follows an old road along the ridge for a while. In the winter, when the leaves are off the trees the views of the surrounding hills and valleys are amazing. I can see how it would look different during spring and summer, and many of the views would be blocked by the trees. This is the flattest walking section of the hike. Once you pass this area the trail is mostly downhill. It is rocky with downed trees and large rocks you have to walk around, or under.

My GPS measured the hike at 3 miles each way from the Centerpoint trail-head down to the Big Bluff Goat Trail. There is about an 1100' elevation change from the trail-head to the Big Bluff Goat

Trail. You can also download the GPX file from our website.

At a little over 2.5 miles into the hike, you will arrive at a campsite and a broad area of bedrock where the trail splits. Take the right fork to head down to the bluff. This is the Big Bluff Goat Trail. The trail will continue downhill and along the bluffs. There is even a hole in the rock that you crawl through to get out on the trail along the bluff.

At the end of the Goat Trail, you arrive at Big Bluff. The bluff is about 550' above the Buffalo River. This is one of the tallest bluffs between the Appalachians and the Rockies.

If you want to hike the trail from Centerpoint to Big Bluff, you should bring plenty of water and some snacks. This is especially important during the warmer months. You should also be in fairly good shape, because the 3 miles back to the parking area is mostly uphill, with some grades above 25%. The round trip took us about 4 hours, and we stopped and had some trail mix and just enjoyed the views at the bluff. Not too bad for a couple of guys around 60 years old!

15
HEMMED IN HOLLOW FALLS TRAIL

GPS COORDINATES

PARKING COMPTON TRAIL-HEAD – 36.08115, -93.30321
HEMMED IN HOLLOW FALLS – 36.07213, -93.30734

Hemmed In Hollow Falls is the tallest waterfall between the Rockies and the Appalachian mountains. It comes in at a height of around 209' tall. The trail down to the falls is steep and rugged, with an elevation change of about 1200'. Most of the trail down into the hollow where the falls are located is downhill. Although there are occasional flat parts of the trail, be prepared to hike downhill most of the way. This also means you will be hiking uphill for most of the hike back up to the parking area.

There are some steep grades coming back out, but if you take your time to stop and catch your breath, and you are in reasonably good shape, it is not that bad.

We left the parking area to begin the hike at 0943, and we were back at the parking area a little before 1400. We also stopped at the overlook about 1.4 miles in and had spectacular views of the Buffalo River Valley and the Falls from across the hollow. The area is absolutely stunning, rugged, and wild.

16
INDIAN ROCKHOUSE TRAIL

GPS COORDINATES

PARKING – 36.08135, -92.56935
INDIAN ROCKHOUSE – 36.09264, -92.57891

The parking area for this trail is located just past the Visitor's Center at Buffalo Point. The Indian Rockhouse Trail has a couple of loop trails if you want to take them to see more of the amazing scenery located in this area..

You can do this trail from the trail-head directly across from the parking area, or you can walk a short distance back up the road toward the Visitor's Center and take the trail-head to the left and start your descent down the trail. I would suggest that this is the best way to hike this trail. I have done it both ways and can say the ascent out of the area is easier starting from the left-hand trail.

The scenery on the way into the area is amazing. Hiking the trail in this direction allows a nice leisurely pace with only a few steep places to descend.

The first thing you will encounter on the way down is a small stream. At the time we visited, there has been an extended dry spell in our area. There was a small amount of water running. I'm sure there is a small spring somewhere up the creek.

After you cross this stream, the trail runs pretty much parallel to the stream down to the next interesting rock formation. The Natural Bathtub is a formation that has worn from the rock over eons of erosion. It forms a natural rock tub as water flows through it.

At this point, we opted to take the upper trail, which turns to the left toward the Rockhouse. This is a large natural rock overhang that provided shelter for early Native Americans while they hunted and gathered food in the area. It is around a half-mile hike from here to the Indian Rockhouse. But don't worry, there is plenty more natural beauty to enjoy on the way.

On the way, you will pass another spring and an interesting rock formation called the sculpted rocks. This is a place where the water has carved intricate shapes into the bedrock, forming a small cascade.

You'll next cross a small bridge on the trail over the stream that formed these rock formations. Then you will be approaching the Indian Rockhouse after a short distance. This is the crowning sight of the hike. A huge rock overhang with duel skylights on one end. On the other side is a spring-fed stream that flows through the back of the shelter. The clear water runs back underground a little further toward the front of the structure. There is also a small cave that is on the backside of this stream. We were lucky that since there hadn't been any rain in a while, the stream was low, and we could cross and look into the small cave.

There are many more sights to see as you hike back out. Once it is time to hike back take the same trail you entered on, and you will shortly come to a fork in the trail. Stay left and take the lower trail to see some different scenery. The lower trail leads back to the area of the Natural Bathtub. Stay straight on the trail, and you will follow Panther Creek for a while. This part of the trail has high bluffs and other scenery to keep your interest. A short hike up this trail will bring you to another, smaller rock shelter. You can go in and walk around inside this shelter too.

After you explore here for a while, you will continue to follow Panther Creek until it meets another stream. This is where you start the climb out. The first part is a little steep, but not bad. You will end up on a trail that follows a bluff line. On this short climb up is where you will encounter an old zinc mine. You can actually go inside and look around the entrance to the mine.

Once you explore the zinc mine, continue to walk along the bluff until you arrive at the bottom of a waterfall. The trail continues under the waterfall, and then you will have a series of rock steps that take you to the top of the falls to continue your journey out.

There is one more sight you will want to catch before you get back to the parking area. The Sinkhole Icehouse is a large sinkhole beside the trail. It is marked by a trail sign.

Once you pass the sinkhole, the trail makes a gentle climb until you arrive back at the parking area.

17
KING'S BLUFF/PEDESTAL ROCKS TRAIL

GPS COORDINATES

PARKING – 35.72361, -93.01523
KING'S BLUFF – 35.72467, -93.02503
PEDESTAL ROCKS - 35.72107, -93.02461

To reach King's Bluff from the trail-head, you will cross a small rock bridge. The sign for the King's Bluff trail will direct you to the right. The trail rises slightly for a short distance and then begins heading downhill. The trail is not difficult and is easy to follow. There are signs along the trail that say "Not Trail" with a red circle and line through it. These signs will keep you on the trail.

King's Bluff is about 0.9 miles from the trail-head. You will come out of the forest onto a wide, flat bluff area with beautiful views of the valley. There is a waterfall to the right. I would suggest that to see the waterfall in all its glory, planning to visit right after a substantial rain in the area is your best option.

You should spend a little time exploring the beauty of the bluff area and enjoying the views. Once you are finished exploring around the bluff, you can take the trail back the way you came, or continue along the loop trail. The sign says that the trail back to the parking area is actually 0.1 miles longer than taking the loop trail out to the left. I would suggest you take the loop trail that follows the bluff area. The rock formations and views of the valley are quite incredible.

On the loop trail you will come to the Pedestal Rocks area. This is a collection of weathered rock pedestals that tower over the landscape. You can leave the trail and climb down among the pedestals to really get an appreciation for these amazing natural rock formations.

A word of caution is needed here. There is a sign that advises that this is a high cliff area. Please stay safe and watch your children if you take them to visit this area. Be safe and enjoy one of the many natural wonders that are so plentiful in the Natural State, especially in the Ozarks.

18
KINGS FALLS

GPS COORDINATES

PARKING – 35.89452, -93.58493
KING'S FALLS – 35.90186, -93.57447

You begin your hike to King's Falls at the parking area on Madison County Road 3500. There is a sign here at the trail-head so the parking area is easy to spot when you arrive.

This is a short out and back trail of about 0.5 miles each way, and the trail is mostly flat. The trail follows the King's River to where the short but strikingly beautiful waterfall is located.

There are plenty of other things to see along the trail. These include an old rock wall and some small rock shelters undoubtedly used in the past by the native peoples who inhabited the area.

If you visit please be mindful that the trail runs along beside private property. Please be respectful of the property owners and don't cross fences in the area.

19
LILES FALLS

GPS COORDINATES

PARKING – 36.05549, -93.17920
LILE'S FALLS – 36.05760, -93.17872

If you are looking for an easy day trip to see a beautiful waterfall while you are in the Ozarks, then Liles Falls should be on your list.

These falls are named for Jim Liles. He was very instrumental in getting many of the hiking trails established in the Buffalo National River area. In fact, the Buffalo River Trail crosses over the top of Liles Falls.

This is a short out and back hike that you can take to see a waterfall on the way to the Erbie Campground.

To reach Liles Falls, take Highway 7 south out of Harrison, AR. About 3 miles north of Jasper, you will be looking for a sign to Erbie Campground. The sign is a little hard to spot if you are traveling south because it is on the left side of the road.

Another problem we encountered was using Google Maps in our search. On the maps view, the road is shown as 79. It is only when you turn on the satellite view and zoom in that the road is labeled Erbie Campground road. Being aware of this should make it a little easier for you to find.

Turning off the highway, the road is gravel but is well maintained and should be easy for even passenger cars to traverse. You will go about 3.5 miles on this road, and you will see a small pull-off area that is large enough to park a couple of vehicles. The pull-off is just after you cross a small stream. This is the stream that feeds the falls. If you see water running under the road, that is a good sign that the falls will have water.

After parking, walk back over the stream, and you will see the trail on the right side of the road if you are facing the same direction as you drove in.

The trail to the falls follows the small stream and intersects the Buffalo River Trail at the top of the falls. The walk to the falls is about 100 yards, so it is easy for all ages. The day we were there we met a couple with a baby and a 4-year-old child. So this is a beautiful natural area that the whole family can enjoy.

When you reach the top of the falls you will encounter a small cascade. This is also where the Buffalo River Trail crosses, and it is a well-marked trail. The cascade is striking in its own right.

Be careful in this area because the rocks have very slippery moss on them. There is a trail heading down below the cascade and to the top of the falls.

This is where the trail gets a bit steep. You should use caution because it is steep and a fall here could risk serious injury. This is not to try and dissuade you from going but just to remind you that this is a wilderness area, and you should always use caution.

On the day we chose to explore the falls, there wasn't an enormous amount of water flowing over the falls, but the view was spectacular just the same.

As you can see from the photo above, this is a stair-step fall and not a straight drop-off. To me, this makes it all the more interesting.

Now that you have seen the photos get out there and enjoy all the beautiful scenery that the natural areas have to offer in the Ozarks. Also, please remember that this is a natural area so if you carry anything in please carry your trash back out. Let's make sure and preserve the natural beauty of these areas for those who may come after us.

20
LONESOME HOLLOW FALLS

GPS COORDINATES

**PARKING – 35.80648, -93.15767
LONESOME HOLLOW FALLS – 35.80466, -93.16016**

If you want to see an amazing waterfall that isn't a long and tiring hike you need to consider Lonesome Hollow Falls. To get to the falls take Highway 7 to Cowell, AR. The turn from the highway is located next to the Cowell Cemetery. The GPS coordinates for the turn-off are 35.82019, -93.16298. Take the road behind the cemetery and there will be a road that bears to your right. Take that road (listed on Google Maps as Taylor Ridge Road 427).

When the road forks stay to the left and continue to follow this road for about .8 miles. There will be a faint road trace on the right with a dirt berm. Park here and cross the berm to start the hike to Lonesome Hollow Falls. The GPS coordinates for the parking area are 35.80648, -93.15767.

Cross the berm and follow the old road trace as it winds downhill. Shortly you'll be able to hear the water crashing over the falls. The coordinates to leave the road are 35.80370, -93.15878. Turn right and climb down below the bluff line here. When you get below the bluff line turn right and follow the bluff to your right a short distance to the falls.

The coordinates for the waterfall are 35.80466, -93.16016. The waterfall is listed at 47' tall and the area around the falls is spectacular. There are also many smaller cascade waterfalls downstream as well.

21
LOWER HORSETAIL FALLS

GPS COORDINATES

PARKING – 35.75247, -92.93816
LOWER HORSETAIL FALLS – 35.75658, -92.94115

Lower Horsetail Falls is found off Falling Waters Road in the Ozark National Forest. You can reach the falls by following what is known as the Horse Trail.

To reach the Horse Trail take Highway 16 at the intersection with Highway 7 from Sand Gap East toward Ben Hur. Turn right onto Falling Waters Road. This road is fairly well maintained, but lower cars may have trouble with it. You will continue past Falling Water Falls (stop and spend some time here because the falls are directly beside the road) and eventually reach a narrow bridge. Park on the other side of the bridge and walk back across the bridge. The Horse Trail will be on the right. This trail generally follows the creek.

Lower Horsetail Falls is a little less than a half-mile down the trail. The trail to the falls is a little hard to see off to the left. A clue you have found it is that there is a short trail to the right leading to the creek and a lovely cascade waterfall that you can walk out on when the creek is low. The trail up to the waterfall is fairly steep, with large boulders littering the drainage. This forces you to scramble up and around them. When you finally make it below the falls the view is amazing.

There is also an Upper Horsetail Falls. We didn't make the climb up there on this trip since it is said to be a much smaller waterfall, and there hadn't been any rain here for some time, so there was little water flowing over the falls when we visited.

Once you finish this short hike you can drive about a mile down the road and [you can see Six Finger and Fuzzy Butt Falls](#) right beside the road.

22
MAGNOLIA FALLS/WOODS BOYS FALLS/HADLOCK CASCADE

GPS COORDINATES

PARKING – 35.86282, -93.38510
MAGNOLIA FALLS – 35.86540, -93.39839

Magnolia Falls is a spectacular 26-foot waterfall that cascades into a tranquil pool of water, offering a serene and peaceful ambiance that will leave you mesmerized. Located near Deer, Arkansas, Magnolia Falls is an easy 2.1-mile out-and-back trail that will take you through scenic bluffs and rock formations, making your hike an unforgettable experience.

    The trail to Magnolia Falls is a little over 2 miles in and out, offering visitors the chance to explore three different falls. In addition to Magnolia Falls, visitors can also explore Woods Boys Falls and Hadlock Cascade, two other waterfalls located in the same area. The hike to Magnolia Falls is generally considered an easy route, taking an average of 50 minutes to complete.

    The Magnolia Falls area is not just about the waterfall; it offers scenic views and stunning rock formations that will leave you in awe. You will get the chance to explore the Upper Buffalo Wilderness, an area that is known for its unique rock formations and majestic scenery. The area around Magnolia Falls is very scenic beyond just the falls itself, with some great bluffs and rock features.

From the parking area on Newton County Road 6, the trail is on the right. There is a Wilderness Trail sign on the left side of the road. This is where you can park. The trail slopes down gently as you pass a rock wall built by early settlers. There are also many natural rock formations to see as you walk the trail. You will come to a small stream and just across the stream are two yellow trail markers that have been nailed to the trees. Take the trail to the left at the fork and Magnolia Falls is a short distance. To visit the other falls, take the right fork down and around the bluff line. Where the bluff line ends, turn left and follow the trail along the bluff line to get to the bottoms of Woods Boys Falls and Hadlock Cascade.

23
PAIGE & BROADWATER HOLLOW FALLS

GPS COORDINATES

PARKING – 36.10520, -93.26795
PAIGE FALLS – 36.10501, -93.26685
BROADWATER HOLLOW FALLS - 36.10282, -93.26602

Paige Falls Trail is a heavily trafficked trail inside the boundaries of the Buffalo National River Park. Paige falls is a short but beautiful waterfall that appears to be spring-fed. It has water flowing even in drier times.

To reach these falls take Highway 43 out of Harrison, AR. The road to reach the falls is marked and the sign will say NC 2660. As you approach the town of Compton the road will be on your left. If you reach the town of Compton you have passed the road and will need to turn around and head back.

This is a county road but a word of caution is in order. The road is not paved and it is pretty rough. My 2 wheel drive SUV didn't have any trouble but I would caution that it probably isn't the best place to try and take that new sports car you just bought.

Follow the road for about 2 miles and you will see some places you can park. Walking a short way further along the road will take you around a sharp bend in the road to a low water crossing. This is the creek that runs down and creates both waterfalls. The trail to the falls will be on your right just on the other side of the low-water crossing. There is also a nice cascade to your left as you cross.

The trail is short and it follows the creek bed which has been carved out of solid rock over the span of millennia. After crossing the creek there are several ways you can reach the falls. You can walk the rocks that line the creek, you can take the high trail which takes you along the creek, or there is a lower trail that takes you between and around huge boulders. If you choose to take any other route than the high trail you will want to circle back to the high trail to get below the first waterfall you come to, which is Paige Falls. This route is easier than trying to climb down the rocks. The Paige Falls trail takes a short but fairly steep fork to climb down to the falls. There are many natural rock formations on the trail. You can walk between huge boulders and the kids will have a blast exploring all the hidden spots on the Paige Falls trail.

The creek shows how water erodes even bedrock over time. Once you have spent time at Paige Falls it's time to see Broadwater Hollow Falls. To reach Broadwater Hollow Falls you will need to climb back up to the high trail and follow it about 200 yards further downstream. The trail will lead down below the falls for a great view. The trail is a little steep and it was slick due to the rain the day we visited. Just be careful and wear good hiking shoes or boots and you should be just fine. Broadwater Hollow Falls is about 21 feet tall and is a cascading waterfall.

The trail is highly trafficked during warm weather. It continues past the falls and includes a spring flowing from a small hole in the rock below the falls. The landscape is breathtaking because of the huge rocks and boulders along the trail, which you can climb over or around to get better views of the falls.

This is a fun trip for the whole family. The hike is short so it isn't too strenuous for the kids and the trail is not too bad for children either.

Broadwater Hollow Falls

24
PARADISE FALLS

GPS COORDINATES

PARKING – 35.88470, -93.37995
PARADISE FALLS – 35.88110, -93.39328

The parking area for Paradise Falls is located beside Highway 21 near Deer, AR. The gravel parking area isn't marked with signs, but it is pretty easy to spot on the west side of the highway.

From the parking area, there is a small berm that you cross to access the trail. It is an old logging road that is mostly grown up. There were plenty of briers to navigate through. I would have to rate this one as a bushwhack since the trail is lightly used and was tough to see with all the downed leaves. Follow the road for a bit and you should see some trail marker ribbons marking the place where the trail turns downhill to descend into the drainage.

Once you locate the drainage it was easy to follow the trail along the creek. There are lots of rock formations, small waterfalls, and cascades to see along the way.

Most people take the trail on the bluff line just above the falls, then take the steep and muddy trail down, using a rope someone tied to a tree.

I have a deep distrust of placing my safety in the hands of a rope that I don't know how long has been in the weather on the trail. If it breaks it could lead to a nasty fall. So we hiked a little further downstream and located a break in the bluff line. It was steep, but not muddy because there was a thick carpet of leaves covering the ground.

Once you make it down to the creek it is only a short hike back upstream to an open area below the falls.

25
PONCA TO STEEL CREEK – BUFFALO RIVER TRAIL

GPS COORDINATES

PARKING – 36.02094, -93.35527
STEEL CREEK CAMPGROUND – 36.03859, -93.34642

To begin your hike from Ponca to the Steel Creek Campground, head to the Ponca low water bridge where the trail begins. From here, you'll embark on a journey through some of the most beautiful terrain in the Buffalo National River area.

This 2.2-mile stretch of the trail is a must-see destination for hikers of all levels, offering stunning views of the river, waterfalls, and rock formations. The elevation gain is about 400 feet over the length of the trail.

Hiking the Buffalo River Trail from Ponca to Steel Creek Campground is a half-day adventure that is sure to leave you awe-inspired. This out-and-back hike is 4.4 miles in total, making it perfect for those looking for a moderate hike that can be completed in a few hours. Along the way, hikers will enjoy some of the most picturesque views in Arkansas, including seasonal waterfalls, panoramic vistas, and towering bluffs.

One of the highlights of this hike is the overlook vista that offers stunning views of the river and surrounding mountains. From here, you'll have a bird's eye view of the Buffalo National River, which is a great spot to take a break, snap some photos, and enjoy the peacefulness of nature.

As you continue on the trail, you'll come across seasonal waterfalls that are particularly impressive in the spring when the wildflowers are in full bloom. Additionally, hikers will be impressed by the rock formations and towering bluffs that add to the beauty of this trail.

At the end of the trail, you'll reach the Steel Creek Campground, which is a perfect spot to relax, have a picnic, and enjoy the serenity of the river.

When you get back to the Ponca Low Water Bridge be sure and take the short side trail to visit the Historic Farmstead.

26
RICHLAND FALLS

GPS COORDINATES

RICHLAND CREEK CAMPGROUND – 35.79731, -92.93517
RICHLAND FALLS – 35.80058, -92.96021

Richland Falls is located in the Ozark National Forest on Richland Creek. This area is a waterfall hiking enthusiast paradise. It contains 35 named falls, with hundreds of smaller unnamed falls and cascades along the creeks in the area. You can get more information and pick up a handy pamphlet showing all the waterfalls at the [Richland Waterfalls Welcome Center](#) in Witt Springs.

The trail-head for this hike is located in the Richland Creek Campground. There is a parking area as you drive into the campground and a small road with a gate to the right. This road leads along Richland Creek up to where Falling Waters Creek empties into it. There is a sign where the creeks meet showing the trail-head

This is the place where it is very likely you will need to make your first water crossing, even if there has not been substantial rain. Twin Falls is a short distance up Long Devils Fork from Richland Creek, and you can follow a separate trail to reach it. This will require another crossing of the creek if you decide to take this trail.

The scenery along the trail is amazing. You can view vistas of the creek valley from far above the creek in some areas, and then the trail will wind down to follow right along the creek bed.

After about 2 miles you will come to the spot where Long Devils Fork merges with Richland Creek. This is where you would need to cross if you wanted to hike up to Twin Falls.

Once you cross the creek it is only about a half mile hike upstream to see Richland Falls. For the best views be sure and visit soon after rains in the area.

Be advised that there are two other trails that can lead you to Richland Falls via Twin Falls. If you choose one of those ways the trail will be a little longer with more elevation change.

The first option is one we took to both falls that is quite steep and rugged, with significant bushwhacking involved. There is a small pull off from County Road 1 where you can start your hike. The coordinates for the pull off are approximately 35.8254, -92.94729.

Be sure you have the coordinates for Twin Falls in a GPS, or you have great map navigation skills if you choose this route.

The other option is to take the trail to Sandstone Castle and continue down that trail to Twin Falls. From there, it is a short distance to Richland Creek Falls.

27
RUSH GHOST TOWN TRAIL

GPS COORDINATES

PARKING – 36.13162, -92.56810

The Morningstar Trail is a 0.3-mile loop trail that passes through the ruins of the Morning Star Mine buildings. This trail is generally considered easy, taking an average of 7 minutes to complete. It is open year-round and is a popular destination for hikers and walkers alike.

The trailhead can be accessed at the Morning Star Trailhead or Rush Landing. For those looking for a longer hike, the Rush Mine Level Trail is an enjoyable 2.8-mile out-and-back trail that provides a mildly challenging hike through a former mining area.

The Morningstar Trail offers a unique opportunity to explore the history of Rush, Arkansas. The ruins of the Morning Star Mine buildings, including a blacksmith shop, livery barn, and smelter built in 1886, are still visible along the trail. Additionally, the Rush Creek crossing and the former mining community of Rush provide insight into the area's rich mining history.

Aside from the historical aspect, the trail is also surrounded by the natural beauty of the Buffalo National River. Hikers can expect to see a variety of flora and fauna, including wildflowers, butterflies, and birds. The trail is also known for its fall foliage and offers a picturesque view of the Buffalo River in the autumn months.

The Morningstar Trail in Rush, Arkansas is a must-visit destination for hikers and history buffs alike. This short but scenic trail offers a glimpse into the area's rich mining history while surrounded by the natural beauty of the Buffalo National River. Whether you're looking for a quick hike or a longer trek, the Morningstar Trail and nearby Rush Mine Level Trail are easy hikes for those looking to view some history of the area and take in the beautiful scenery surrounding the Buffalo River.

28
SANDSTONE CASTLE

GPS COORDINATES

PARKING – 35.84177, -92.98434
SANDSTONE CASTLE – 35.81645, -92.97269

The Sandstone Castle is a popular sandstone rock formation located in the Richland Creek Wilderness area of the Ozark National Forest.

You begin the trail to Sandstone Castle at the roadside. There is a small blue sign up a small embankment listing the distance to Sandstone Castle as 2.4 miles. It also lists the distance to Twin Falls, which is in the same area, as 3.7 miles. The first few hundred yards of the trail are the most difficult. There is around a 16% grade uphill for several hundred yards as you climb above the road below. Once you reach the bench of the hill it is a flat hike for the most part.

If you take the hike to Sandstone Castle in the winter with the leaves off the trees you can see more of the surrounding valleys and landscapes. I'm not sure how much you could see in summer because the forest is dense along the trail. Several overlooks along the way give views of the valleys below of Richland Creek and Big Devil's Fork.

Once you arrive at Sandstone Castle you are treated to a fantastic expansive view of the valley and the hills of the surrounding countryside. Use caution near the bluffs because they are high and steep. A misstep here could result in tragedy. This warning is not to discourage you from visiting this amazing place, but to just use caution as you would in any rugged outdoor area.

The trail continues along the bluff for a short distance where you can go down and explore the bluff shelters below. There are several shelters that were most likely used by Native Americans in the area in the past. One shelter even has a rock fire ring near the entrance so it is apparent that some adventurous people have hiked in and spent the night in the shelter.

Once finished exploring the area you can turn around and hike back out to the trail-head. You can also continue downhill to see another scenic wonder of this area by visiting Twin Falls.

If you are planning a trip to the area a great way to see multiple scenic wonders might be to take two vehicles and station one at the Richland Creek Campground and bring the other to the Sandstone Castle trail-head. Hike to Sandstone Castle and then continue downhill to Twin Falls. Then you can make the short half-mile hike to Richland Falls before you continue on to Richland Creek Campground. Then you can drive back to retrieve the other vehicle from the trail-head

There are numerous additional waterfalls and hiking trails in the Richland Creek area. Be sure and check out our posts on Falling Water Falls, Six Finger Falls, Terry Keefe Falls, Lower Horsetail Falls, and Punchbowl Falls.

29
SIX FINGER & FUZZY BUTT FALLS

GPS COORDINATES

PARKING – 35.76155, -92.93710

Six Finger Falls is another of the many waterfalls that can be visited in the Ozark National Forest. This part of the National Forest, near Witt Springs, AR has thousands of acres of wilderness. It is also the perfect terrain for waterfalls.

Six Finger Falls is one of 36 waterfalls listed on the brochure I have from the Witt's Springs Waterfall Welcome Center. If you plan to visit I highly recommend stopping in for a brochure. If you are camping in the area they have hot showers and other amenities. They are supported by donations.

This waterfall can be seen from Falling Waters Road a short distance after you cross the concrete bridge over Falling Waters Creek. The falls will be visible on the left. There is a small pull-off for parking.

There is a short rocky trail down to the waterfall. The trail is about 50 yards and leads out onto the bedrock that creates this unique and picturesque waterfall. The water has eroded the bedrock to produce channels that run between outcroppings in the bedrock. This results in the appearance of fingers protruding into the creek. When the water is low you can walk out and over the rocks to a short trail on the opposite side of the creek. This short trail leads to Fuzzy Butt Falls.

Once you cross over Six Finger Falls the trail to Fuzzy Butt Falls is easily seen. The trail leads to a small box canyon a few hundred yards down the trail.

In the rear of the canyon, you will find the 16' waterfall named Box Canyon Falls, also known as Fuzzy Butt Falls.

30
SMITH CREEK NATURE PRESERVE

GPS COORDINATES

PARKING – 35.93470, -93.38637

Located in the heart of the Ozarks, this preserve is a haven for outdoor enthusiasts, hikers, birders, and those seeking a quiet escape from the hustle and bustle of city life.

Imagine a place where you can wander through a pristine forest, listen to the babble of a clear creek, marvel at cascading waterfalls, and watch rare wildlife in their natural habitat. All this and more can be found at Smith Creek Nature Preserve in Arkansas.

Nestled in the heart of the Buffalo National River Valley, Smith Creek Nature Preserve is a hidden gem waiting to be explored. With its rugged Ozark terrain, lush forests, and pristine waterways, this nature preserve offers a wide range of activities for visitors of all ages and interests.

Smith Creek Nature Preserve features over 10 miles of hiking trails that wind through dense forests, along the banks of Smith Creek, and up to stunning waterfalls. The trails are well-marked and range in difficulty from easy to moderate, making them accessible to hikers of all skill levels. One of the most popular trails leads to Elise Falls, a beautiful cascade that is particularly impressive after a heavy rain.

Smith Creek Nature Preserve is not only a beautiful place to visit but also an important conservation area. The preserve is home to one of the largest colonies of Indiana bats in Arkansas, which hibernate in nearby Sherfield Cave during the winter months. In addition, the preserve is a haven for a wide variety of other wildlife, including rare birds, fish, and reptiles.

31
STEELE FALLS

GPS COORDINATES

PARKING – 36.01323, -92.19170
STEEL FALLS – 36.01795, -92.17934

Steele Falls is a waterfall many people have not heard of. It is located in the Ozark National Forest near the Gunner Pool recreation area. If you've ever visited Blanchard Springs near Mountain View, Arkansas you were only a short distance from this hidden gem.

At around 60 feet, Steele Falls is one of the taller waterfalls in Arkansas. The water pours over the side of a bluff and onto the rocks below. It appears the stream that creates the falls is spring-fed since the creek we crossed to get to the falls was dry above where the creek from the falls flows down into it.

My GPS measured the total for the hike at 2.9 miles with a little over 400 feet of elevation change. The trail is an old abandoned forest road. Just keep following the road down until you reach a creek bed. There will be a trail sign on the far side of the creek. Follow the trail up the small drainage a few hundred feet and you will be below Steele Falls.

It appears there is a trail running around the bluff line. There may be a way to get above the falls if you feel like trying to find it.

The hike out is mostly uphill, with a few flat spots on the trail. Although it is uphill most of the way out, the grade isn't too steep, and we only stopped to shed jackets and another time to talk to a couple of people we met on the trail going in as we were coming back out.

32
SWEDEN FALLS

GPS COORDINATES

PARKING – 35.96962, -93.45273
SWEDEN FALLS – 35.97146, -93.45917

Sweden Falls is a tall waterfall located in the Sweden Creek Natural Area near Kingston, AR. Sweden Falls is the 5th tallest waterfall in Arkansas at 81' tall. Of course, the tallest waterfall in Arkansas is Hemmed in Hollow Falls. The area around the falls is typical for this area of the Ozarks. Large boulders, tall bluffs, and deep valleys are everywhere you look. This one can be viewed from the top by taking the left trail where it splits. Taking the right trail at the fork will take you to the bottom of Sweden Falls and down into the creek bed along a bluff line.

    To reach Sweden Falls you take County Road 9 to the south off of State Highway 21 between Kingston and Ponca. The road to the area is fairly rough so a high-clearance vehicle is recommended. No need for four-wheel drive on this road. Just be aware that in this rocky terrain, the roads are extremely bumpy. Slow speeds are the order of the day when trying to reach the trail-head

It was a pleasant surprise to find a new gravel parking area marked with cables just a few hundred feet further up the road from the gate where people started the hike in the past. This lot is level and is in great shape. The trail is well-marked from this spot and is fairly well-used, so it shouldn't be a problem staying on the trail.

Once you leave the parking lot the trail is downhill for the most part. The first thing you will encounter is the trail intersecting the old trail coming down from the gate you passed on the road in. Stay to the left here and continue downhill. After a short distance, you will encounter an old home place that is in fairly decent condition considering they are abandoned buildings.

After exploring around the old homestead, continue down the trail a short distance and the trail will fork. The trail to the left leads to the top of the falls and the trail to the right descends to the bottom of the falls along the bluff line. We took the trail to the bottom of the falls first. You will have to scramble over and around some rocks, and the water seeping from the side of the bluff will be dripping down from above. In spite of this, the trail is not difficult, and you won't get too wet.

The trail ends at the falls and you are looking up 80' to where the water flows over the rock ledge at the top and crashes onto the rocks below. You can walk behind the waterfall under a rock overhang that was almost certainly used by Native Americans for shelter when they inhabited this area.

After you explore around the bottom of the falls you can now head out the way you came. Follow the trail back up to where the trail splits off. You can continue out to the parking area. However, I highly recommend you hike the trail along the top of the bluff to the top of the falls. There are some amazing views of the surrounding area and the bluffs that run along Sweden Creek.

Once you get to the top you will be treated to amazing views of Sweden Falls.

Please be careful in this area as the rocks can be slick if they are wet from the rain. The bottom of the creek is very slick when the water is running too. There are no safety rails so be sure and keep a close eye on children.

Now you can start the hike back to the parking area. Just follow the trail back along the bluff line until you intersect with the main trail then start your hike uphill back to the parking area. The trail from the parking area to the falls is around 1.5 miles. Hiking to the top of the falls will add around 1/2 mile to that. My GPS said 2.3 miles, but there was some walking around exploring, so

I'm going to say 2 miles total.

    I would recommend this hike for those looking for a fairly easy hike to see a waterfall. We saw several people with children on the hike and I would say it is kid-friendly.

33
SYLAMORE CREEK HIKING TRAIL

GPS COORDINATES

BARKSHED RECREATION AREA – 36.01923, -92.24983
TRAIL-HEAD – 36.01918, -92.24903

This is a small camping area with primitive sites for camping. The road is very narrow, so I wouldn't recommend pulling anything larger than a small pop-up camper, or a small off-road camper like the one my friends purchased. This area is best suited for tent camping.

North Sylamore Creek runs clear and cold past the campground and eventually empties into the White River near Mountain View, AR.

We took a short hike from the Barkshed recreation area down the trail toward Gunner Pool. We planned to only hike a couple of miles of the trail since it was getting warm and humid fast as we finished our coffee and prepared to head out.

The trail access point is on the road to the campground. This well-traveled trail is quite easy to follow. The trail follows the bluffs above the creek for the 2 miles we hiked in and back out. The scenery is beautiful, with plenty of rock formations and views of the creek along the trail. The photo below is of my friends who were hiking with me.

We climbed down from the trail into a drainage at one point and hiked down to the creek to see the amazing scenery. The views were just stunning.

In my opinion, the Barkshed recreation area has a lot to offer if you like to get off the beaten path and visit an area that isn't too crowded. It offers clear, cool waters in North Sylamore Creek. It has rugged natural beauty. It offers hiking and a primitive camping area. It is a great place to get away from it all and relax.

34
TERRY KEEFE FALLS

GPS COORDINATES

PARKING – 35.76548, -92.93336
TERRY KEEFE FALLS – 35.76582, -92.92458
CALYPSO FALLS – 35.76280, -92.92590 (APPROX)
SPLASHDOWN FALLS – 35.76268, -92.92548 (APPROX)

Terry Keefe Falls is a short hike off Falling Waters Road in the Richland Creek area of the Ozark National Forest. The hike is a little over a mile out and back to the parking area. This short hike is very scenic, with tall bluffs to one side and a small drainage to Falling Waters Creek on the other.

The trail-head for the falls is a little over .3 miles past Six Finger Falls on the right. There is a place to pull off Falling Waters Road on the left. Terry Keefe Falls is in a box canyon similar to Fuzzy Butt Falls. The falls are 78 feet high, so it is one of the taller waterfalls in the area.

Remember, this area is literally in the middle of nowhere. Be sure and download maps you may need, as cell service is almost non-existent in this area.

Terry Keefe Falls is pretty easy to find even without a map. As you start down the trail you will cross the Ozark Highlands trail around mile marker 41. Continue to follow the trail you are on, keeping the bluffs to your left and the creek to your right. You will come to a point where the creek turns left. You can stay on the trail if it is wet, or just follow the creek bed if it has been dry

I would rate this as an easy hike. There is very little elevation change, and until you get to the creek the trail has gently sloping areas that are not tough and are easy to navigate. Beware of the slick rocks as you near the falls. They can be treacherous, so watch your step. This is a fun and easy hike with a tall and impressive waterfall at the end. This is one for the kids to enjoy too. There are no steep bluffs or other places they would need to be careful of.

TWO ADDITIONAL WATERFALLS

You have the chance to see two more waterfalls while you are hiking Terry Keefe falls. As you make your way back from the waterfall you will notice another small creek drainage to your left. If you travel up that drainage there are two more picturesque waterfalls you can visit.

This is a little more of a challenging hike but the results at the end are worth the effort. Make your way upstream in and around the creek bed to see Calypso Falls.

Next you need to cross the creek and climb up and around a large boulder to reach Splashdown Falls. This waterfall can be seen if you look closely upstream past Calypso Falls.

The climb up around the boulder is quite steep and slick. Use caution when making the climb. Once past this area you can walk upstream on the rocks between towering shale bluffs on one side and the creek on the other.

The view of Splashdown Falls from beside the clear pool beneath it makes this effort well worth it for the payoff at the end.

35
TWIN FALLS - CAMP ORR

GPS COORDINATES

PARKING – 36.05658, -93.25763
TWIN FALLS – 36.05464, -93.25809

To reach the falls, you take Highway 7 out of Harrison, AR. Take a right off Highway 7 onto Highway 74 near Jasper, AR. Camp Orr road is approximately 6 miles from the turn onto Highway 74.

Twin Falls is obviously the most spectacular when there has been substantial rain in the area. It is best to visit during the wet season in the Spring or Fall, or right after a substantial amount of rainfall. You may also see good water flow the day after a thunderstorm.

I would be remiss if I didn't warn you about the steep road to reach Twin Falls. This road is not recommended for low passenger cars or the family mini-van. When there is a sign on the side of the road warning you to stop and let your brakes cool before going any further, that should give you an idea. We actually stopped twice to let the brakes cool, even though I was only using them when absolutely necessary.

When you arrive at the parking area, the trail to the falls is well-marked and well-worn. In the wet season, you can hear the falls as soon as you get out of your vehicle.

Walk the trail that follows a small stream for about 400 yards to the bottom of the falls. There are a couple of other trails you can follow that branch off of the main trail. One of these trails will take you to the top of the falls. BE CAUTIOUS if you venture to the top of the falls because there are no safety rails, etc. The rocks can be very slick and a fall from up here would not have a good ending.

36
TWIN FALLS – RICHLAND CREEK

GPS COORDINATES

RICHLAND CREEK CAMPGROUND – 35.79731, -92.93517
TWIN FALLS – 35.80570, -92.96412

Twin Falls in Richland Creek Wilderness is a true natural wonder. The falls are formed where two creeks – Big Devils Fork and Long Devils Fork – merge into one creek. Each of the falls is from a different creek falling into the same watering hole. It is a challenging hike to reach the falls, but the reward is more than worth it.

The Twin Falls Trail is a 2.8-mile one-way hike that is considered strenuous due to the bushwhack and the creek crossings it requires. The trail is located in the Ozark National Forest Ranger District: Big Piney Sub-Location: Richland Creek Wilderness Region. The trailhead can be found at the Richland Creek Wilderness NF Campground, and a short side trail leads to Richland Falls, which is also worth a visit. The whole area is very scenic and offers plenty of opportunities for nature photography.

To get to Twin Falls, you will need to follow Richland Creek and climb bluffs. A short side trail leads to Richland Falls, and after that, you will need to continue west following Long Devils Fork for a short distance until you reach Twin Falls. It's important to note that the hike to Twin Falls requires a strenuous hike and several creek crossings.

It is important to wear sturdy shoes and bring plenty of water for the hike. The trail-head is located at the Richland Creek Campground.

When you reach Twin Falls, you will be rewarded with a beautiful natural wonder. The falls are 17 and 19 feet tall, and they occur where the two creeks merge. The water flows into a small pool at the bottom, which is perfect for swimming on a hot summer day. The falls are surrounded by beautiful rock formations and lush greenery.

37
TYLER BEND PARK HIKING

GPS COORDINATES

PARKING – 35.97591, -92.76507
BUFFALO RIVER SCENIC OVERLOOK – 35.97890, -92.77218

Tyler Bend Park is a beautiful destination located in the middle district of the Buffalo National River near St. Joe, Arkansas. The park offers a range of outdoor activities and scenic trails for visitors to explore. Among the park's attractions are the Collier Homestead and the Buffalo River Overlook Trail.

The Collier Homestead is a historical site located in the Tyler Bend area. It was homesteaded by the Collier family in 1932 after they moved from Kentucky. Today, visitors can take an easy walk to the homestead and see what life was like for early settlers in the Ozarks. The homestead is also accessible via the Collier Homestead Trail, which takes visitors along the river and atop the bluff above the river.

The Buffalo River Overlook Trail is a scenic trail that offers amazing views of the Buffalo River. The trail is a short one, spanning only 0.1 miles, but its location on the bluffs above the river provides breathtaking panoramic views of the valley below. It is one of the shorter trails available in Tyler Bend Park, but it is an excellent choice for those who want a brief hike with a stunning payoff.

    The Riverview Trail at Tyler Bend Park is the longest of the Tyler Bend Trails. This trail is 2.1 miles. It is considered moderately challenging and gives visitors a chance to explore the park's Ozark forest while enjoying sweeping views of the Buffalo River. The Riverview Trail also takes visitors to the Collier Homestead by way of the Buffalo River Overlook.

BONUS ATTRACTIONS

ALTHEA SPRING IN OZARK COUNTY MISSOURI

GPS COORDINATES

PARKING – 36.64252, -92.22601
SPRING – 36.64200, -92.22737

If you enjoy finding out-of-the-way places then a day trip to Althea Spring is just what you are looking for. Althea Spring is the 23rd largest spring in Missouri. And when I say it is an out-of-the-way place, I mean out of the way.

Althea Spring is just up the hill from Patrick Bridge in the Patrick Bridge Conservation area. The spring bubbles up from the rocks in the hillside and runs downhill into the North Fork River. The spring emits a flow of about 12 million gallons of water per day or around 19 cubic feet of water per second.

There aren't many towns close by. Drive down Missouri Highway H until you reach the bridge. There is a parking area on the west side of the road. Walk up the hill a short way and you'll reach Althea Spring.

The water that is discharged from the spring is a deep blue. In the stream that is produced by the water flowing from the spring, there is an abundance of plant life that thrives in the cold water filled with nutrients.

If you follow the stream a little further you will come upon the waterfall that is formed by a concrete dam that was placed in the stream. This was used as a source of power by Karl Schmidt. Mr. Schmidt designed a power system that used the flow of the spring to generate electricity for the home he shared with his sister.

If you continue to follow the trail downstream you will find where the stream from the spring enters the North Fork River. The North Fork River in this area is known for its trout fishing. To find out more about the trout fishing opportunities in this area you can read this article on the Conservation Federation of Missouri website.

Patrick bridge over the North Fork River is a single-lane concrete low-water bridge. It becomes impassible in times of high water. Caution is advised when crossing the bridge since it is only a single lane.

The North Fork River in this area is rugged and scenic. Float trips are available on the river, and several outfitters are in the area. In case you were wondering, yes this is the North Fork of the White River that becomes Norfork Lake in Arkansas. Below the dam, at Norfork Lake, the river joins the White River and eventually flows into the Mississippi River in southeast Arkansas.

If you decide to visit the area a good map will serve you. Be advised that due to the mountainous terrain cell phone reception can be spotty.

2
ARKANSAS GRAND CANYON

GPS COORDINATES

PARKING – 36.64252, -92.22601

Arkansas' Grand Canyon may not be as deep as the one in the western US, but the views of the valley are stunning nonetheless. Located along scenic Highway 7 just a few miles south of Jasper, AR. you can pull off the highway and catch the views on your drive. This roadside area has a gift shop, observation tower, and ample parking to get out and stretch your legs while admiring the beauty of the Ozark countryside.

The parking area is 2,100 ft. above sea level. The lowest part of the valley is about 1,000 ft. below on average. On most days, you can see into Missouri, which is about 40 miles to the North. Looking from end to end of the valley takes in 50 miles. You can see about 1.3 million acres when looking out across the valley.

Get more information on Arkansas Grand Canyon. Check out our page on the Buffalo River near Jasper, including a video. Check out some other things to see while in the Jasper area.

3
BEAR CREEK OVERLOOK

GPS COORDINATES

OVERLOOK – 36.41166, -93.09441

Bear Creek Overlook is located on Dubuque Road in Boone County, Arkansas. It is not marked and can be hard to spot. The only hint is that the road is a little wider where people have pulled off to the side. Caution is advised if you decide to see this. It is a steep bluff and there are no guardrails or safety guards here.

The Bear Creek Overlook has an amazing view of Bear Creek as it winds toward Bull Shoals Lake. You can check out our tour of places you can visit on Bear Creek.

Bear Creek begins at Bear Creek Springs, north of Harrison, AR. You might even see a bald eagle when you visit. They seem to like dining on the trout as much as people do.

4
BLUE SPRING HERITAGE CENTER

GPS COORDINATES

OVERLOOK –36.46569, -93.81300

Blue Spring Heritage Center in Eureka Springs, Arkansas is full of natural beauty and history.

To reach Blue Spring Heritage Center, follow US Highway 62 West out of Eureka Springs to County Road 210. There will be a sign on the right showing you where to turn.

Once you reach the Blue Spring Heritage Center, you can park in the large parking lot. You enter the grounds through the gift shop and pay the entrance fee. The fee was $9.75 per adult, $6.50 for kids 6-17, and free for children 5 and under when we were there. The grounds are also wheelchair accessible, so everyone can enjoy this attraction.

Once you leave the gift shop, you will see a large waterwheel. This water wheel is a representation of the way the mills at the spring used waterwheels to harness the power of the spring. There were both grain mills and a sawmill at the site in the past as settlers moved into this area of the Ozarks.

Walking along the wooden stairways and paths, you see gardens with native plants and wildflowers everywhere you look. Many of the plants are labeled.

As you descend the stairs, you'll see a rock overhang that was used as a shelter near the spring. This was used by early Native Americans as well as the later settlers that came to the spring. These natural shelters are abundant in the Ozarks region.

As you continue toward Blue Spring, there is a gazebo along the lagoon. You can stop here to rest in the shade or watch the trout swimming in the cold, deep water.

Continue a short distance further and you come to Blue Spring. The spring is surrounded by a wall that is planted with flowers. The red flowers contrast beautifully with the blue color of the spring water.

The spring discharges about 34 million gallons of water per day. The water is a constant 54 degrees. You can feel the coolness of the water when you get close to the spring. There is a walkway over the discharge chute where you can bend down and place your hand into the water and feel how cold the water is.

The spring is also ringed by gardens with natural plants and wildflowers for you to enjoy. The colors of the different flowers in the garden are really something to see.

Once you have enjoyed pausing at the spring, you can continue along the path on the other side of the lagoon. More wildflowers and native plants await you along the path. You may also hear boats on the White River, which is only a short distance from the spring. In fact, the water from the spring flows out to join the White River. This water eventually makes its way from the Ozarks all the way to the Gulf of Mexico. The water travels down the White River into the lakes along the river before it travels all the way to southeast Arkansas to join the mighty Mississippi River.

On the path out you can also see the rock garden. This is an example of the natural rock formations which occur all over the Ozarks.

Before you leave, be sure and visit the heritage center on your way out. There are displays of archaeological items as well as historical items from the area. There are also videos that show the history of the spring and a dive which explored the spring.

5
BLANCHARD SPRINGS

GPS COORDINATES

SPRING – 35.95894, -92.17555
CAVERNS – 35.96387, -92.17928
MIRROR LAKE WATERFALL - 35.96354, -92.17099

    Blanchard Springs Recreation Area is located in the Sylamore Ranger District of the Ozark-St. Francis National Forest in Arkansas. The area is known for its breathtaking spring, stunning waterfall, and well-maintained hiking trails. Blanchard Springs Caverns is a magnificent limestone cave system. Be sure and check whether the caves are open if you plan to visit. The Mirror Lake Waterfall is a beautiful sight located in the recreational area, which has an easily accessible trail to view the waterfall. There are wooden walking paths built along the lake and the stream below the waterfall. Mirror Lake above the waterfall is popular for fishing .

    Visitors can take a stroll on the paved trail to witness Blanchard Spring gushing as a waterfall from the hillside and swim in the clear waters of the North Sylamore Creek. The area also offers several well-maintained and well-marked hiking trails, perfect for visitors to explore the natural beauty of the Ozark woods, ranging from an hour-long to a weekend-long hike.

6
CITY ROCK BLUFF

GPS COORDINATES

PARKING – 36.10161, -92.18564

City Rock Bluff is a hidden gem that is located in Calico Rock, Arkansas. Calico Rock is known for its calico-colored rock bluffs that rise majestically above the White River. Many people drive by the road to City Rock Bluff as they travel down Highway 5, without realizing the easy access to this stunning view high above the White River.

City Rock Bluff is located at 881 Culp Rd, Calico Rock, AR 72519. It is a short drive from downtown Calico Rock and can be easily accessed by car. The location is also marked on Google Maps, making it easy for visitors to navigate to the overlook.

7
GRAY SPRING

GPS COORDINATES

PARKING – 36.17185, -92.68072

Gray Spring near Yellville, AR is a natural spring that discharges from the Ozark Plateaus aquifer system.

Local people use the spring as a water supply. I can confirm that because on a visit to Gray Spring we encountered a young man who was backed up to the spring with a 1,000-gallon water tank in the back of a pickup truck. We talked to him for a while and he said that he makes the trip several times a month to the spring for his mom. He told us she doesn't have city water and they use the spring water for all their household needs.

The spring is actually further in the hillside. The water flows from the top year-round.

Although this spring may not have the natural beauty of some other springs you may see, it is still worth visiting if you are in the area. The water is cold and clear. You should fill a water bottle while you are there and enjoy the refreshing taste of real natural spring water.

8
GRINDER'S FERRY

GPS COORDINATES

PARKING – 35.98431, -92.74449

Grinder's Ferry is a popular swimming hole and canoe launch site on the Buffalo National River. Grinder's Ferry is located between Marshall and St. Joe, Arkansas, on US Highway 65. If you are traveling from central Arkansas, take US Highway 65 North from Conway. The turn-off to reach the parking and gravel bar is 10.6 miles north of Marshall on the right, just before you cross the bridge. From St. Joe on US 65 South, the turn-off is 5.1 miles on the left immediately after you cross the bridge.

The popularity of Grinder's Ferry results from the easy access to the Buffalo River. You can walk across the gravel bar from your car and you are at the edge of the water. Camping is allowed here and there is no cost to camp. Swimming is also popular; many people swim here during the hot summer months. In addition, Tyler Bend park is only a short distance to the south. Tyler Bend is a popular camping and float area on the Buffalo National River also.

The Buffalo River is known nationally as one of the most beautiful scenic float destinations anywhere. From towering bluffs to white water during the wet season, the Buffalo River has something for everyone. During the summer when rain is scarce the Buffalo becomes a tranquil stream. It is during this time that many intrepid adventurers head to the Buffalo to launch canoes and kayaks for a peaceful float trip down the river. There are numerous places to rent canoes and kayaks, or you can bring your own.

The history of the area is quite interesting. During the late 18th and early 19th centuries, the area was a hotbed for lead, zinc, and copper mining. Unfortunately for the miners hoping to strike it rich here, the metal ores in the area appear in clumps and not veins of ore. The unique geology of the area accounts for this. Normally miners find a vein of ore and then continuously mine it. In this area, miners would find a clump of ore, mine it out, then have to go find another clump of ore. This made mining extremely difficult in the area.

The towns of St. Joe and Gilbert are each only a few miles from here. These towns sprang up due to the mining in the area, and the Missouri and North Arkansas Railroad ran through this area. The railroad shipped mined ore and agricultural products north to Springfield, MO. The town of St. Joe has restored the historic railway depot in town. You can visit the railroad museum while you are there as a fun side trip.

Just to the south along US 65 is Tyler Bend Park and Campground. The park has a ranger station, camping, hiking trails, and river access also.

9
HODGSON WATER MILL

GPS COORDINATES

PARKING – 36.70978, -92.26692

The Hodgson Water Mill near Dora, MO. is a nice place to stop, stretch your legs, and view a historic structure. The mill is built atop a spring that flows from the rocks below the mill. In the late 18th and early 19th centuries, the Hodgson Water Mill was an important part of the community in this area of Missouri. The Hodgson Water Mill is a restoration of the original mill that stood on the site.

According to what I could find online about the mill, it was constructed around 1897. In the 1860s, a mill was built on or near the current site. This mill was closed down during the Civil War and it is not known for sure if the original mill survived the war, or if a new mill was constructed.

The spring that powered the mill when it was a working mill discharges approximately 23.5

million gallons of water per day. The spring comes out of the ground below the building and was used to turn the water wheel that drove the grinding machinery. The spring now discharges out and runs by the wheel, then continues out to a small pond in front of the mill, where a small retaining wall was built to create the pond. This wall creates a small waterfall that is a great spot for photos.

A short way down the creek created by the spring is a bridge over the creek. This is also a popular spot for photos while visiting the mill.

If you are in Arkansas, you can drive to Mountain Home and take Highway 5 North into Missouri. When you reach US Highway 160 you will take a right. After several miles, you will make a left turn on MO Highway 181. You will see the mill on your right. It is right beside the highway, so you can't miss it.

10
MAMMOTH SPRING

GPS COORDINATES

PARKING – 36.49581, -91.53550

The city of Mammoth Spring is nestled along the Arkansas/Missouri border in North Central Arkansas.

We visited Mammoth Spring State Park to view the spring. This is a huge spring that bubbles up from underground at the north end of the park. According to the signs posted in the park the spring emits an average flow of 9.78 million gallons of water per hour. So the average amount of water flowing from this underground spring is about 235 million gallons per day.

All of this water flows from underground and across two outflow areas into the lake created by a dam on the south end of the park. The dam was used to redirect the flow of water through a hydroelectric generator in the early part of the 20th century.

Start your tour directly behind the visitor center. This is where you can see a bridge support from the old bridge that connected the train station to the city of Mammoth Spring. The original bridge was made of wood. It was replaced by a steel bridge in later years. The steel bridge was privately owned and was sold for scrap back in the 1960s. In the photo, you can see that freight trains still pass the train station, which also contains a museum.

As you continue north along the path to the spring you will see an old artillery piece to your left. Known locally as the "Big Gun", the sign placed with the gun tells about it's history. It is fired at dawn and dusk each day during the annual week-long celebration known as the "Reunion of the Blue and Gray". This celebration is held annually in July.

After you view the "Big Gun" continue north along the walking path and you'll come to Mammoth Spring. If you've been to other small natural springs you'll marvel at the amount of water that comes to the surface here from underground.

Continue along the path for a short distance and you will come to another bridge that gives you a good view of the second outflow from the Mammoth Spring. The roaring water gives you an idea of how much water is emitted from the spring.

Be sure and take the path to your left up to the raised viewing platform. From there you can get a sense of just how large Mammoth Spring truly is.

You can follow the trail back down the way you came to the walkway and continue around the lake. This will take you to the train station and museum that you could see across the lake from the visitor's center.

The trail around the lake is a loop trail. As you continue from the train station you will arrive at the dam and the old hydroelectric power plant. The dam was built in 1888 to provide water power to drive machinery for local industry. The rights to the dam were bought in 1925 by the Arkansas-Missouri Power Company. In 1927 the hydroelectric plant was built. It provided electricity to the area until 1972.

Before you leave be sure to visit the friendly folks in the Visitor Center and pick up a drink, snack, or souvenir.

11
PEEL FERRY

GPS COORDINATES

ARKANSAS SIDE – 36.49001, -92.79446
MISSOURI SIDE – 36.49442, -92.78022

The Peel Ferry is the last publicly operated ferry boat in the state of Arkansas. It crosses a section of Bull Shoals Lake because there is no bridge connecting the two sections of AR Highway 125. This is something you should see if you are in the area. It operates on Highway 125 crossing Bull Shoals Lake between the Highway 125 Recreation Area and The Buck Creek Recreation Area.

According to the Arkansas Highway and Transportation Department, there were 17 ferry boats operating in Arkansas in 1968. They go on to say that only 4 were operating in the state in 1986.

In fact, one of the 4 operating at that time was in south Arkansas County across the White River on Arkansas Highway 1. I still remember riding that one. It was a much shorter ride than the ride across Bull Shoals Lake on the Peel Ferry.

The Peel Ferry was put into place when the dam was built on the White River to create Bull Shoals Lake. Without a bridge, the people on either side of the lake would have to make an almost 100-mile trip through either Branson, MO, or Mountain Home, AR. So, in addition to being a unique attraction for the ride across the lake, the ferry also serves a valuable function for the people who live in the area.

Many motorcycle riders take the loop on Highway 125 for the scenery and to experience riding the ferry.

From either Mountain Home or Harrison, take AR Highway 62/US Highway 412 to Yellville. In Yellville, you will turn onto Highway 14 to Lead Hill. This road is scenic, but it is also a steep and winding road. There are deer to contend with at times when traveling Highway 14, so be on the lookout. You'll see a sign on your right for the junction of Highway 125. Turn right onto Highway 125 and follow it to the ferry. There is also an Army Corps of Engineers campground just before you reach the ferry landing.

Depending on when you arrive, you may have to wait for a while for the ride across the lake. According to the article linked above, the ferry is a 40-minute round trip. If you were to arrive just after the ferry has left the dock, you might have a wait. But I assure you the scenic ride across the lake is worth the wait.

The other great thing about the ferry is that it is operated by the state and there is no fee to ride the ferry. So this is a unique thing you can do on a scenic drive through Arkansas and Missouri which doesn't cost a thing other than the fuel you burn.

ABOUT THE AUTHOR

Gary Davis was born and raised on a farm in East Central Arkansas. Growing up he spent many hours outdoors hunting and fishing.

He spent his career in the medical field as a registered respiratory therapist and Cardiopulmonary Director. When he retired from medicine in 2018 he moved to the beautiful Arkansas Ozarks.

He has also been a professional photographer and now focuses on photography of all the amazing natural beauty of the Ozarks.

He spends most of his time fishing and exploring the Ozarks hiking and chasing waterfalls. He posts all those adventures on his website called Lost in the Ozarks.

Made in the USA
Columbia, SC
29 July 2024

39569233R00059